MARIAPOSA

POEMS OF LOVE AND LIBERATION

I0620510

MARIAPOSA

POEMS OF LOVE AND LIBERATION

◆ ALMA ROSA AZUL ◆

RIOT OF ROSES
PUBLISHING HOUSE
SEJATNGA
UNCEDED TONGVA TERRITORY
SOUTH WHITTIER, CALIFORNIA

MARÍAPOSA:
POEMS OF LOVE AND LIBERATION

Copyright © 2025, Alma Rosa Rivera

ISBN (paperback): 978-1-961717-27-5
ISBN (ebook): 978-1-961717-28-2

Cover Artist © Richard Castor, Rich Westkoast, elaykidd.wixsite.com, 2025

First Edition, 2025

To request permissions, you may contact the Publisher at riotofrosesllc@gmail.com

Printed in the United States of America.
www.riotofrosespublishinghouse.com

For booking information, *visit www.Almarosaazul.com*

Cover design by Rich WestKoast
Layout design by Waseem Aziz
Edited by Annalicia Aguilar and Anastasia Helena Fenald
Editor-in-Chief Brenda Vaca

For everyone fighting for a new world
& for the girl who yelled,

"More Molotovs!"
at one of my poetry readings.

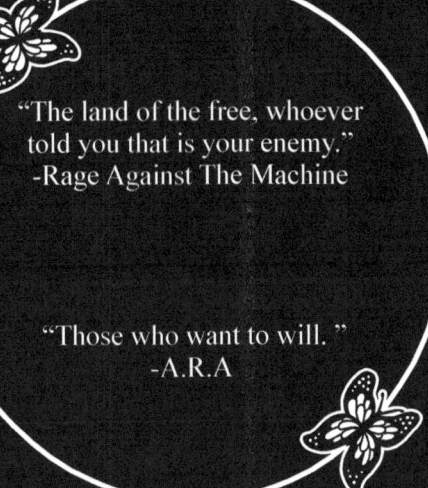

"The land of the free, whoever
told you that is your enemy."
-Rage Against The Machine

"Those who want to will. "
-A.R.A

CONTENTS

MARÍAPOSA

MARÍAPOSA

My

people

dream

of

migrating

like

the

monarch

This
is
the
way
it
was
for
generations
and
generations
before

They are mothers
and children
and fathers

Their dreams were held in their breath
and in their backpacks

Their dreams had wings you know
Some of them tried to cross
and got their wings wet with water though
and the wings got too heavy and so they drowned

Someone who looked like me

eyes

and hair

and skin

Her body
and her dreams
drowned

I wish I could have lent her my wings for a day

I would have liked to have seen her
spinning
a r o u n d & a r o u n d
in the sky
where they couldn't reach
to build a wall

I would be laughing from down below
cheering!
watching La Migra yell at her
shaking their fist and butterfly nets
and she will never come down

She will
live in the sky
till her braids turn gray

Maríaposa

She will make a new life on the clouds
and eat them
like cotton candy

MONARCH

When
I'm
with
You

everything
e x p l o d e s
inside
of
me

It feels like
when *thousands*
of monarch butterflies end their migration
and they sit on branches and just *chatter chatter chatter*
celebrating
because they're *all*
in community

I feel
I feel in community with you
at home with you
Yes
You feel like
Armfuls of orange and black wings

Soft and sweet
A flutter of feelings when I'm with you
You look at me
and my first thought is:
Oh
just *squeeze* my heart till *all* the petals
fall
off

But your body
is one I can hold
and yet never capture
and maybe
I love you so much
I would never think to do so

I'll just watch you
on my finger
and love you there
Until
you
fly
away

AFTER I DIE

I used to think that I wanted to come back as a butterfly

After

I

Die

Perhaps become a swallowtail
the size of a fist
or maybe
r e i n c a r n a t e
as an ocean-hued monarch

But now I know
I'd rather come back
as *Rebellion*
As Rebellion cocooned in an empty bottle
Watch it be thrown
grow wings
explode
free the people
free the world
Yes, I'd rather come back as Rebellion

I'd rather come back
as a bullet
or a jug of justice
or as a mischievous little creature
that makes the gas run out of buses filled
with detained freedom fighters

I'd rather come back as Rebellion
I'd rather come back as
a balaclava mask
or as an obnoxious megaphone
or as a banner dropped
waving hello to freeway drivers down below
Yes, I'd rather come back as Rebellion

I'd rather come back as a cardboard-turned-political sign
or a garbage lid-turned shield
or as an angry nail that pops the tires
of corrupt police cars
Yes, I'd rather come back as Rebellion

I want to come back
as flame
as wind
as freedom
as rage
as a whole uprising

I want to see what the new world is going to look like
Even if it happens decades after I am gone

I don't want to come back
as a butterfly
anymore
A selfish life that would've been

Now
I only want to come back
as a Molotov
with wings

BEFORE THE REVOLUTION COMES
After The Last Poets *When The Revolution Comes*

Before the revolution comes

> They will tell you
> to stay calm
> and carry on
> Tell you to vote
> Tell you to save
> d e m o c r a c y

Before the revolution comes

> They will say
> Fight for your country
> They will feed your children
> propaganda like cereal
> Feed them a false pride for a country
> who is more blood than justice

Before the revolution comes

> They will tell you
> To clock into work
> Stay clocked into work
> Don't unionize your work

Put your back into it
Until you are too tired
To think of revolution

Before the revolution comes

They will call this normal
The people not making enough to live
The people stealing food to live
The people waking up early
to wait in line for food
The people walking
Busing
Driving cars
they can't afford to fix
Pay the tags on
Pay the tickets for
Driving illegally

Everything is *i l l e g a l*

Before the revolution comes

The food being sold on streets
Sleeping on the streets
Selling your body on the streets
Everything is on the streets
Because Americans can't afford

to have a place called home
even though all the homes are empty

Before the revolution comes

The baby formula will be locked up
The children will be locked up
The freedom fighters will be locked up
The good people will be locked up
The bad people will be driving down the street
with wind through their hair
blaring the lights of this country
And those will be the last colors
you will see
before they pull you over
to kill you

They'll say
the body cam was turned off
Call it an accident
Call you crazy
Or deem it a suicide
They'll call it a
Sandra
Bland
Suicide

The slave drivers' star is the same shape
It just goes by a different name
Before the revolution comes

Before the people's revolution comes

The earth's revolution will come
She will set everything aflame
She will be the first protestor
She will pull a Stonewall
be queer about it
And throw the first brick

Before the revolution comes

The revolution
will call on
ordinary people
People like
You
And
Me
To suddenly be extraordinary
and spread this very message
with our entire hearts:

The revolution has come!
The revolution is here

The revolution is alive
The revolution is ready
The people are ready
Are hungry
Are ready to break chains
Are ignited
The people are no longer afraid
Of when the revolution will come
The people will have each other
The people will care for one another
The people will organize
The people will pray
The people will grow
The people will train
The people will teach the children
that good will always win
The good people will always win

The people will trade their fear for knowledge
Trade their fear for arms
Trade their fear for community

The night before the revolution comes it will be quiet

The sound of organizing
Is silence
Is planning

The night before the revolution comes
you will be able to hear a butterfly landing on a leaf

Before
the
revolution
comes

And
when
the
revolution
finally
comes

You will not be able to hear

Your hearts panic
Your hearts beating
Your hearts fear
anymore

BURN (STAY IGNITED!)

People liked me better
when I was nice
e a s y
to
d i g e s t

When I became radicalized
a fight ignited in me!
People became afraid

But the native people
have always burned the land
to keep the earth
healthy
intact
flourishing

So I'll gladly stay aflame
ready to burn away
anything
that isn't healthy
for this earth
or its people

MARÍA VS. MACHISMO

UN MACHO NAMED GUADALUPE

Somewhere in México
there's a man named Guadalupe

A woman's name to many
feminine
not the way our men are raised to be

"Ponte Macho!"
Be tough!
He has always been told

He nurtured his relationship with leather
since childhood
It came in the form of a whip
a whistle sound and then a crack on his behind

When he grew up he wrapped this belt around his waist
Unbuckled it
When he found a beautiful woman
he could rough around
and then he whipped her when she protested
When she questioned his ways
whipped her like he learned as a child

Deep down
all he wants
is to be
soft
This man named
Guadalupe

A woman's name traditionally
He has never been allowed
to indulge in any of the *feminine*
Only his name

When he is alone
he rubs his face against his horse's
He feels every hair against his cheek
He feels safe in this affection
This affection with someone
who can not speak
who can never share his secret
his secret craving for love
to be held
to breakdown
to cry like a child
without the scolding to "be macho"
to be a man
to drink it away
to numb all feelings

Somewhere
In México
and in the United States
and everywhere
there's a man named *Guadalupe*
In my lifetime
I have met many
a brown man
wearing his manhood on his back
Since boyhood
Since always

And for just one day
he would love to find
the farthest place on his land
where no one can see him

and set it down

DEMONIOS

We are young brown girls at a party

the women wear their prettiest heels
the men have shirt buttons opened
and hearts closed—

We sit in the back of a truck telling stories
of weeping women
and drowned babies

For us kids
tamarindo candy
the moon
and tales of witches
was always a good time
Always witches
Always bruja stories

At night
when the fiesta comes alive
The sound of accordions
and maracas fill the dance floor

Hips shake
Brown hands cinch a woman's waist

The party becomes a creature
It's heart resuscitated
by the stomping of boots and heels

then the drinking begins

The men flock
as the bottles are opened

There is tequila and so many beers
that they form them in a circle around them

The men fumble
Spanish slurs
They are bewitched by poison

their sombreros
are taken off their heads
and

Horns
sharp spines
and claws
emerge from brown skin

The eyes…
The eyes always become
something foreign

dark and raged
We are children
watching the men
we respect
become monsters
our Papis
our Tíos
Abuelos and Primos

This is the real *folklore* of México
These are the demons
that traumatize our children
that kill our women
that grabs holy matriarchy by her wrist
and tosses her to the ground

I've learned through my ear
against the wall
that our women are the piñatas
that get broken
after the party
That stays broken
for generations
and generations

by the men
and the alcohol
and the machismo

and the unhealed trauma
that disguised itself

as a handsome man at the party

only to be later exposed

as Satan himself

his
hooved
feet

dancing to a
cumbia
b e a t

MACHETE

The señoras
I grew up watching
Lived their lives like shields
Alchemizing arms
from brown to metal
To protect their bodies
And those of their children

> *Year after year*
> *Bottle after bottle*
> *Bruise after bruise*

Eventually the señoras
Grew up to be

> *Tired*
> *Enraged*
> *Hurt*

And the men
Wake up one day
Looking to their left
Wondering why
Their wives
Became swords

MEXICAN REVOLUTION (DAISIES FOR BABIES)

My Bisabuelo
  fought in
    the Mexican
      Revolution

The war left him
blood hungry
and
violent
A brain altered
with images
of blood and bones

He beat on my Abuelo
and then my Abuelo beat on my Papi
and then my Papi beat on me

In my family
the men passed down
a bandolier of
m a c h i s m o
so the violence from the civil war never ended
The enemies just became children

and the guns became fists

I don't want to be a woman
who continues to wage war
on the ones I love
so
I give a daisy
to a laughing baby

And point the barrel
at an unjust government instead

MACHISTA

Machista!

You are not an eagle
or a nopal
or a snake

You are not a flag for all women
to pledge their allegiance to

So why don't you use those two little legs of yours
and serve your own damn plate

MARÍA MOLOTOV

MOLOTOV

I am a red flag
He waves a black
and—
he doesn't love me

I wish he would think about me
even just a little
I like the way his lips move when talking of revolution
or when they kissed me
The two felt like very similar things

But most of all
I like
the way he carries
a burning M o l o t o v for a heart

I want so badly—

(even if it were the end of me)
To put my hands
on his chest
To feel the
W a r m t h
and then the
E x p l o s i o n

35

of what it could feel like
to be in love with him

DANDELIONS

I didn't know him when he was in prison

I wonder
what
he
was
like
back
then

He talks soft like tiptoeing through a sentence
or maybe like he's been hurt enough

If I knew him
I would've written to him

I would have liked to have sent him a poem
in exchange for a pen drawing
of an Aztec princess
or maybe I would have sent him some radical books
A stack of books
with words so powerful
they could have demolished
all of the concrete around him

All I know is
I would've tried

I would have tried
to make him feel loved
to make him feel
remembered

I would have sent
a bouquet of dandelions
through the cracks
near his feet
just so he had a reason to smile

VALENTINE'S DAY

R e d

M	ake
A	merica
G	reat
A	gain

C a p s

We snatch them off the heads
of the modern-day colonizers

Place them in the shape of a heart
and set them on fire

This
This is my revolutionary
Valentine's card for you
my love

All of the ugly parts of myself
and this world
on fire

FARCE OF JULY

The hood doesn't love 4th of July

The hood loves
BBQs
and days off
and anything that disguises a gunshot

The hood doesn't love 4th of July

The hood loves
cold beer
and seeing the family
and having a few hours
once a year to stop
and look at the sky

The hood doesn't love 4th of July

The hood loves
sleeping in
and laughing with friends
they never have time to see
and any moment just to breathe

The hood doesn't love 4th of July
Farce of July
red
white
and blue

The real hood doesn't love this holiday
doesn't love this country
doesn't love this country that lies to us
that enslaved us
and disguised it
as saving us

The real hood knows
is tired
Every year we say:

"It's hard to be a proud American when…"

Brown children are in cages
or
When they overturned *Roe vs. Wade*
or as we are funding bombs
on Palestinian children and people

I sit here wondering
what will be America's failure next year
Next month
TOMORROW

The hood doesn't appreciate America
doesn't love America
4th of July is just a paid sick day
to deal with all the sick things
this country does to us and the entire world

This holiday
just a day given off
so we all have the energy to wake up the next morning
and clock in
for another year
of this country's mediocrity

BLOOD LUNCH

Everyone my homie except Capitalism/Capitalism is green light worthy/ It/ The poet's poison/ Destroyer of community/ Let's curb stomp Capitalism/ Booted and bloody/ No love songs/ No butterflies/ Capitalism is/ killer of dreams/ of health/ of sleep/ killer of relationships/ of love /of peace/ Destroyer of breath/ of mind/ of family / Capitalism is greed/ Capitalism is always hungry/ Always taking from the starving/ I want to tell it/ to open its mouth/ Wide!/ Let me see every single one of its sharp bloody teeth/ and let me feed it /a big fat brass knuckle sandwich

JUSTICE 8

For the Justice 8- Till all 8 come home

Victorville Courthouse

They put our activists on trial there/ When they came out the sound of chains shaking was new for my ears/ so my brain registered it as the sound of "losing freedom"/

I didn't see any of them cry/ This/ the only moment
that I was grateful for Machismo/ Grateful for the way construction is ingrained in Chicanos/ The way we all know how and when to make our face into brick when absolutely necessary

We witnessed them/ Took time off of work and from the kids just to witness them/ The courthouse seats filled with activists and community members/ Blessed in jade and feathers/ Braided tight like sweetgrass/ We kept our faces straight as our friends and family became political prisoners/ accused of/ Terrorism/ Conspiracy/ Assault

We became brick for those hours

We didn't want the judges or the police to see us weak or sad/ That's a kind of vulnerable you have to earn from a brown person/

My people don't deserve to be caged

Not the Justice 8/ So I hope to one day see them free again/ The remaining 7[1]

The only orange hue on their backs/ a sunrise/ and their arms filled again with the warmth of their children

---

1   Author's Note: At the time of this writing only one member of the Justice 8 was released. Edin Enamorado remains in prison as the last of The Justice 8.

AQUATIC ANARCHY

It's time for change!
even the ocean
is revolting!

Is organized
Is resisting

In its waters
Orca whales are splashing
symbols of Anarchy
Hitting rudders
to drown the boats of
oceanic oppressors

They do this in pods
in community

Strong marine formations create successful sinkings
When the female whales become grandmothers
They head the pod and spread the knowledge

May their storytelling live forever!
May the stories of their rebellion
be passed down to their children

and may we do the same
in our fight
against all
oppressors

DIRTY DOCS

I wear dirty Docs
everywhere I go

Black boots with
faded yellow stitches
A symbol of resistance
of commitment
If they could speak
they would say one sentence:
We are ready!

Ready for action
Ready to protect a street vendor
or a woman on a street being harassed
Ready to take down surveillance cameras
or march in a protest

Dirty Docs
These aren't worn to be pretty
A tool for liberation
A tool for my feet
To give me speed
Give me wings
To lift up this body
That carries my fire

Everywhere I go
And in these streets
I stay ignited
With chin up
Looking up at a cloud
Sending out a prayer
To a god I don't have a name for
But I love
And believe in
And I tell them
To please protect me
And protect all of us
Who are out here
Pulling up our bootstraps
Ready to do the

Fighting
The organizing
The building
To create a new world

MOLOTOVS ARE AS PRETTY AS BOUQUETS

Molotovs are as pretty as bouquets to me

A beer bottle becomes a vase
To a flame-turned-red rose
Smell it before you throw it
Swoon over its sweet aroma

In your nostrils
The greatest fragrance to be discovered
This
The smell of the people's liberation
This
The smell of a resistance that will never die

LA MARÍA EN MIGRACIÓN

HOMERO, REY DE LAS MONARCAS

*For Homero Gomez Gonzalez
and all environmental activists murdered*

They called him
The King of the Monarchs
because the sky around him
was always a confetti of butterflies

He was
raised in a family
of wood makers in Michoacán, México
His family chopped down the monarch's habitat
so they could afford their own

One day
a monarch sat on his cheek
He decided that day to be their protector instead
He lived a good life dedicated to protecting
la monarca and its habitat
His throne was made
of wood and Asclepias

He left a party one day
and then went missing
He was found unwinged

His soul that made him beautiful
flew elsewhere
It was the part of him
they couldn't put their hands on

What an unfair death!
Homero,
You could not make a fist
because your palms
were always full of butterflies
Rey con alas
Rey de Monarcas

I hope you know Homero,
That the Monarch still migrates every November
And I believe with all my heart
That you are in the sky
wearing orange and black wings
flying alongside them too

STRETCH MARKS

You live with a girl from México
Both of you
are pregnant
She is here to anchor her baby to a country she hopes will provide
for her
You are worried about your children learning Spanish
Yearning to smell the soil of a country you've never been to
What a funny thing how life is
México and California
In reality are just two balconies with lovers sighing over their
ledges
Dreaming of getting to the other side
Each side, a different desire
A different fantasy
The only difference is the way we word the feeling
We call it dreaming
Y ellos soñando

Fingers clasped between borders
I imagine them
Playing
RockPaperScissors
Doing a Chicano Handshake
anything
but letting go

ODE TO WOMEN NAMED MARÍA

When you are brown and pregnant
people will tell you
"Name her anything but don't name her María."

This name
for some
smells more stench than fragrance
It's ancestral sound
reminiscent
of old beat up huaraches
or of a wise Indígena woman
her skin aged into
deep waves

María
they say your name
sounds like beans brewing

María
they say your name
looks like the border and the wall

This makes them think of
the people Donald wants to push behind the wall and how they
don't want to be one of them
How all they want is to pass the checkpoint they feel
Every time a white person looks at their skin too long

At night,
black hair spreads apart on her pillow
and in the moonglow
the dream is always one of being American.

So they avoid being Marías
They want to forget the sound of the rooster's crow
They choose their middle names instead
and what a sad way to live
to not love the very root of where you grew from
to not be proud of how your name sounds like the ocean
or of how it blooms out of your mouth
like a bouquet of roses

María Cósmica

María Bonita

María María

Alma Rosa Azul

I hope you remember that for many
your name feels like home

Named after a woman
so loved
people walk on their knees to see her

BLACK FLAG BUTTERFLY

Monarca!
You are
Anarchist
of the sky!
Crossing la frontera without papers
like our people have always done before

MARÍA MAYBE IN LOVE

MEXICAN MONUMENT

He reminds me of all the things
I love about Chicano men

Sharp jawline
and chiseled muscles
He's built like a monument
Strong and Brown like penny bronze
So gorgeous
You can't help
but stop and stare
as you walk on by

I want him to always shine
never to rust
with the bitterness of heartache
so I
rub up against him

with hands
mouth breast

rub up against him

with legs
toes breath

Alma Rosa Azul

I want to swing a hammer
at all and every colonizer's statue
but for him
I'd polish his feet
until he breaks free
from his pedestal

to grab my waist
and give me a kiss

CLOUDS

Watching Edgar

from the window of the house

running
down
the
hill
of
y e l l o w
f l o w e r s

He
a little brown boy
my mom would watch
when we were children
Me and my little chest sighing
A tiny hand pressed against the glass

I have always loved the men of my culture

I'm a sucker for the way

Their skin
Their eyes
Their hair
Look against the
c l o u d s

BROWN SUMMER

"Don't go into the sun,
you'll get too dark."
They forgot that our ancestors
were the people of the sun
That we are also of the earth
which means we are like plants
always growing the most beautiful
in warm places
and in the unexpected

In an act of defiance
I walk through the streets
soaking in the heat waves
I become darker and darker
and I know that that's okay with you
For brown on brown love is essential
For brown on brown love is revolutionary

Our love
I know it could last forever

For how can we not know of romance
of fast heartbeats

when both of our skins
have been so
deeply
kissed
by the sun?

CREATION OF LOVE

I hear
that in Italy
the tourists gather at the Sistine Chapel
cameras, phones, and mouths open to see man and god
touching fingers

Ah! What a spectacle
I heard it took Michael sixteen days as
it was the most complicated of all the paintings in the Vatican

But somewhere in a little Oaxacan restaurant
You and I sat
A Mexican masterpiece
feeding one another sweet mole,
sips of café de olla, and little bits of potatoes
and no one took pictures
and no one encapsulated us to last forever on a ceiling
and no one stood up and cried
"Bravo, what a marvel!"
And yet we were
My hand holding tortilla
and the tortilla that touched your
lips
and your lips that touched my heart
and at that moment

Ah! We were such a bold creation of love
Much higher than
Adam
or fingers
or God

1,000 ROOSTERS

I saw you walking
through the door
and my heart rose

Serenading
with the song
of
one thousand
roosters
crowing

The roosters
tired of blood
tired of fighting
helped one another
untie all the razor blades
that were roped onto their ankles

They begged
all the machista men
that kept them captive

to let them be
Pacifist
Buddhist

Poets
instead

so that we could
spend all the hours
of the day together
staring at you
falling in love

I WAITED FOR LOVE

I waited for love
on the train
and the coffee shop

I waited for love
in front of a fountain
and outside
in front of a string of lights

I waited for love
at the bookstore
and the poetry reading
and the bookstore again

I waited for love
at the museum
and the aquarium
and at a show in a crowd of people
who are all trying to look different
so they all look the same

I waited for love

Alma Rosa Azul

I waited for it everywhere
Then I found it
and I looked for it again

MEXICAN AMELIE

Romantic
Nostalgic
Neurotic

I
am
all
of
them
since
the
day
you've
left

Will I ever find another person that felt like *You*?

MARÍA Y EL MAR

BLUE AZUL

An empty marisco restaurant
A shrimp with its head still on sheds a tear
Oysters like La Llorona seek their stolen pearl
Fish like Antionette
beheaded
I thought we'd see all
the beautiful parts of summer together
Always said, "I hope we will make it till summer."
But now it's just me
Alone
Deep Whales
B l u e
A z u l
Wondering how many sirens
call your name
now that I'm not near

BLUE WALLS

I painted my room
cobalt blue
the summer
you left me

the air
filled with floating jellyfish
the bed
a giant clam to crawl into

all day
all night
tear drops
pearlescent

I let every wave of memory
crash into me
destroy me

on delusional days
my hand and head leaned against the walls
dreaming they were the ocean
and that you and I were

Maríaposa

swimming together
in a sea
of blue paint

THE TEAR

I touch myself
to feel an ounce of love
but feel nothing

Immediately afterwards
a long tear drop falls from my eye
A hot pearl of loneliness
that gives more relief than my fingers

This thought comes out

"There is no one out there for me to love."

There is no one out there for me to love
There is no one out there for me to love

I force myself to say

"There is no one out there for me to love… yet."

I want to be held more than anything

not by someone attractive
or someone I like
or someone I like the idea of

I want to feel *love*

I like the crazed feeling of being lost in someone

Without the feeling
life just feels like waiting
Feels like wearing
a large heart watch on my wrist
ticking ticking ticking
I wait for the hands to hit midnight
To point to somebody new
whispering
"Him "

Instead it beats
and beats
and beats
with a pounding that sounds like

"Not
yet..."

SEAWEED

I want to submerge myself underwater
and never come back up

Take me where the seashells and seaweed get spat out

Let the Ocean reject me too

I want to know if it hurts
just as much
or less than a man

IT OCCURS TO ME: I AM THE BROKEN HEART AND LIMBS OF GODDESS COYOLXAUHQUI

After Sandra Cisneros, from *Woman Without Shame*

Do not come knocking on the door of my heart
Heartache and suitors
leave!

I want alone
This heart guarded by nopales and
roses, more thorn than petals

So much better
Solitude
Lonely
Then the highs and lows
of what eyes could do
Much better quiet
or the sound of a wax candles crackle
of wax spinning
Let my love be selfish today
Maybe forever!
Let my love be
a closet of ocean blues
and Mexican embroidered dresses

Let my love be
hot baths and freshly born books

I don't want to hear
anymore
sweet nothings
Give me instead the sweetness of pan dulce
And the sound of the teapot
howling! howling!
Steam
Let the teapot blow all its steam
Let it scream!
I just can't take any more of it from a human

Closing every eyelid of the house
Merlot thrown back till it hits the molars
Sweating out of every pore
Cursing under every breath
Copal smoking heavily

One
last
thing

I want you
No longer
a part of me

UNTITLED

I've written enough poems about you

even my pages
curl their edges over their ears
and run away from me

MARÍA MEXICA

MI PUEBLO

My people

They
are
beautiful
to
me

Heavy hooped
Ocean eyeshadow
and a
brick smile

My people

They
are
beautiful
to
me

On every corner a traveling tianguis
A bouquet touching the sky
The bell that rings throughout summer

My people

The
Border
Breakers

Their skin so stunning in the sun

Their feet so quiet in the night
My people
the brave
No papers No problems
(Actually lots of problems)
But my people the humble
The hard workers
Always looking for ways to earn their dollar
and always thanking god when they figure out how
My mami
My ancestors
My Mami and all the generations of prayers that always
protect me
All the Mamis
Who we should respect like Creator because without them we
are nothing

I love my people
That tend so sweet the children
and the strawberries

The bus stoppers
The car hoppers
The Papis with their thick hands
The women with our thick blood
I love us all

The way we buzz and swarm like busy bees

The way we're sweet
The way we sting

CHICANO PARK

Chicano Park/ When they built you/ they planted seeds of resilience into the soil/ so the trees they grow in the shape of fists here/ and the air the people breathe is filled with resistance like no other/ Chicano Park! /The first museum of the Chicano/They mad dogged the bulldozers away/ said a park will be laid here instead/San Diego/ Barrio Logan/ Barrio of the people who loved their culture so much/ they tattooed their stories/ their faces/their grito/their victory/onto the skin/ of their city

LAS CHICANAS CHA CHA

Chhh
Chhhh
Chicannna
like Chhhhh
Chhh
Chicana
like
Chhh Chhh
Chisme y la Chamba
Chicana like Chhh Chhh
Cholitas
basking in
their glory
Chhh Chhh
Chicana like Coyotes being a part of your family's story!
Chhhhhhhh
like Chillona along the river
Chhhhhhhh
we always share the story of la Chillona
always show mujeres like Chillonas y Chhh Chhh Casadas y y y
Cocinando
y Cuando queremos ser gritonas
Cuando queremos ser Chingonas
son los hombres quién nos ponen el dedo
a la boca y nos dicen

"Chhhhhhhh
ya no hablas
Chhhh"
much more beautiful quiet
the men of our CULTURE tell us!
you tell me Chhh like Comal
like mami can you put another tortilla en el Comal
Chhhhh like carne sizzling
Chhhhh on the stove
jalapeños feos
Chhhh on the stove
but when I think of Chhhh
I think of Chh Chh Chicana
and I think of Calaveras
and Chh Chhhh all of las Chicanas will one day become Calaveras
and Chhh Chhh all that will be left is our herstory
so I say Chh Chhh
mejor te Calles
porque Chh Chh yo soy el Cambio
Chhh Chhh
y el mundo
Chhh Chh mujer Con Fuerza
Chh Chh sin verguenza!
porque yo soy Chh Chh Chicana
Chh Chhh y Chillona
Chhh Chh Corajuda
Chhh Chhh y Cabrona
Chhh Chhh Callejera

y
y
y
Cualquiera

yo soy muchas Cosas
pero Chh Chhh
primero Chhh Chhh
siempre yo soy
Chhh Chhh
primero yo soy
Chhh Chhh
siempre yo soy
primero yo soy
Chicana

HUIPIL DEL MUNDO

The world is like a Huipil
like Mexican embroidery

From the surface level
a rainbow of Otomi Creatures
and colorful flowers

This the Consumerism
The social media
The beauty industry
The push for individualism

But turn it inside out
and you will see
the entanglement of
knots and strings

The Genocide
The Capitalism
The Greed
The Pollution

The world can feel
A heavy place
But let us find beauty

even when the world is ending

I want to embroider
a message of love
to you real quick

This is it
"Keep going.
The world is tough,
but you are so much stronger."

COLUMBUS THE PIMPLE

I wake up with a big pimple on my face
On Indigenous People's Day
The skin underneath conquered by bacteria
The colonizer in this story
maybe falling asleep with makeup on that one day I was too tired
to wash my face
or maybe
just the stress of capitalism

But pimples sometimes come and eventually they go
Just like Columbus
and his statutes
and his holiday

Maybe that pimple created by creator
so there's more of me
Taking up space
A fist raised up in the air
on Indigenous People's Day

SEÑORA X CORE

I want to grow up to be old
I want to grow up to be wise
I want to grow up to be a señora

A modern take of the classic
I'll trade
all rosaries for poetry
and
Catholicism for Anarchy

I'll walk a xolotl and
Chill with cholos
Down mezcal
And be down for the cause
When I grow up to be a señora

When I grow up to be a señora

I want to be
ungovernable and
unpredictable
I want to whisper into my plants and then shout into the youth

to fight the system and not their urges
And that masturbation is *a wonderful and normal thing*

When I grow up to be a señora

When I grow up to be a señora
I want to have the funniest jokes
and share my best sex stories

be the loca with a loud ass cackle
With blue
Or gray
Or box black
hair
Maybe missing teeth
But never missing out on personality

I want to grow up to be a señora
grow up to be an elder
a grandma to
Activists
And queers
And young punks
And anyone who never felt at home
I want to grow up to be loving
I want to grow up to be radical
I want to grow old and tell the youngsters
What did or didn't work when we organized
back in my day

I want to be the señora

with the best tamales
The best pozole
The best consejos and
The most wisdom

She's inside me
I don't want to kill myself anymore
because I would like to reach her
To know her
To see her in the mirror one day

I dream of being a señora now
A radical hellraiser filled with rage and words
And when you see me walking down the street
Move to the side
Because nothing
and no one
will stop me

MARÍA THE POEM, MARÍA THE POET

ME, YOU & POETRY

There is nothing more erotic
than a man who can write a good love poem

Don't give me red roses or blue violets
Tell me about
how you want to love me so bad
you'd bleed all of your sins out of you for me

Obsess for me
I like a man who can love me till insanity
Write me
wild primitive hungry poems
That make me want to peel off all my clothes and skin
Till we are just vessels
Just hearts
Let's play with words and body parts
That
Kind
of
Poem

Write me a poem
That is radical
Destructive towards the government
Volcanic

Dangerous
Write me a poem that empowers me so much
it can be read at a protest
At an uprising
A poem that can change the world

You do believe that don't you?
That you could do that with a poem,
Change the world?
Believe in poetry the way that I do
Or don't come around at all
I don't want watered-down words

Turn me
into an old-fashioned with mezcal
or the moon
or a songbird
Turn me into a metaphor or a simile
Cause what a relief that would be
To be cradled into your pages
Dressed in Times New Roman
And be anything but me
Give me a break from this body
From this world
From this humanity
Just me and you
Just you and I
Just me, you, and poetry

ONCE

I once loved a man
Who would
talktalktalktalktalktalktalktalkTALK!
His vocal cords were the harp to my heart
He spoke in poems
and stories
Nothing was ever worded simple
Everything intertwined
with talk of magic and fables
He taught me
that the weight of words
was worth as much
No!
worth more than gold
and I've been carrying that lesson
in the treasure chest near my heart ever since
I miss him
I miss talking to him
I miss the talk of poets
poetry and books
His eyes were filled with pages
Those eyes and when they looked at me
how they felt like flocks of quetzales in my stomach
Break all the cages!
I'd let all my feelings fly with him

Alma Rosa Azul

He loved me
And I loved him
He loved me
and he loved others
I loved him
But not how he needed
He loved me
But I couldn't give more

I loved him
Some days I still do
He's somewhere out there
missing or hating me
That's okay
It changes every day for me too

I'm still trying to write him out of all of my poems
But I manage to put him in all of them instead
Even if it's one word
The last ember
The last of the flame

We had a great romance of poets
When it ended
I always say god applauded
Because what we had was

Truly
something
special

I'm glad I once experienced love
I'm glad I once experienced special
even if that word hurts heavy now
Once

I AM A POEM

I am a poem
A big poem
A big spirit with a big mouth
I talk and sometimes it's hard to stop
A flood of jokes and play on words,
Words are fun to play with you know
A jungle gym on line paper

I am a big poem
A "little brown woman"
He would call me that
Him a large milk-skinned lover
And I enjoyed being a drop of cacao
A stroke of brown paint against him
I am a big poem
Actually just a poem
Not a girl
Or a human
A vibration
An energy that can not be stopped
Even if you tried
And like all energy
It exists everywhere
And is everything
And is nothing

I am a big poem,
A heavy spirit with light pockets
A rebel yet
A servant to this little big big art form
Called POETRY
Let it chain me to the desk of commitment
Then release me
A frenzy
An animal
Wild
A wild wild poet
That's who I am
Release me from all borders
institutions
and rules
Release me from all labels
arrangements
and systems
Let me live the life of a poet
A painter of words
And I will die happy this way

YOU BRING OUT THE REVOLUTIONARY IN ME

After Sandra *Cisneros' You Bring Out the Mexican in Me*

You bring out the revolutionary in me
The organized chaos in me
The precolonial
pre-settler wild in me
The I was Xochitl
before Eve in me
The smoke cleanse baptism
New beginning in me

You bring out the revolutionary in me
The insurgency
And then the urgency
For love in me
The destruction of property
The building of community with me

You bring out
The 1312
A
C
A
B

In me
Spell amor with a circle A in me
You bring out the revolution in me
The people power
Pueblo power
Freedom fighter
Take the streets in me

We could do it together
You
and Me

The land given back
The empire crashing down
The crushing of capitalism
No borders
No cages
Fight till we're free

Don't you think?

You simply
Deeply
Beautifully
Bring out the
The revolutionary in me

Now
Won't
You
Please

Fall asleep
holding me

ANOTHER CHICANA POEM

I grew up Catholic
so everything I did was a sin
I was given a list of commandments to tame me
So I became an explosion instead
A rebellion naturally

My mami
She sings to church songs
She says don't pray any other way
My friends
they dance in a whirlwind
of feathers and copal
I think to myself
to pray twirling
is so much more beautiful than on your knees

Everything about me is spiritual
Is hermanahood
Is Xicanisma
Is María mayhem
Everything about me community
Everything about me brown

Alma Rosa Azul

I am my parents' sequel after they crossed the border
They raised me to be the best American so I became a
mediocre Mexican instead
Speaking Spanglish
Pocha pronunciations
Even the white things about me
are brown I promise you that

I grew up knowing
my motherland through souvenirs
Grew up knowing Family members through pictures
The border has always been the villain in all of my people's stories
I write the stories of my people who don't know the words for all
of their feelings

I once fell in love with a poet
He told me
"Everything about you feels like a poem."

I need you to understand
Everything about me is poetry
Everything about me is ocean, art
Spoken word for me is music
I go to a book signing
and have a poet sign my book like a pair of breast
I believe that one day I will be the one signing

Maríaposa

I wish I believed in organized religion
But nothing in an artist's life ever seems to be organized
But I do believe in many other things

I believe that those with the least
are always the ones who give the most
I believe seeing a monarch butterfly
means you're going to have a good day
I believe that the way you make people feel
after you leave a room says everything about you
I'm okay with people remembering my spirit but forgetting my
name but if you'd like to know
My name is Alma Rosa
My veins run from San Luis Potosi, México
All of my poems are for México
All of my poems are about a country
I've only heard about
All of my greatest loves are the people
that came from it and their children
From the Mission to Boyle Heights
to Barrio Logan and Barrio Fuerza
I am my culture's greatest admirer
All of my poems little love notes
To my parents' country
Just to say

Alma Rosa Azul

I want to get to know you
I adore you
I long for you
and that
so many of us on this side of the border
are missing you

ACKNOWLEDGMENTS

There are those who I love; friends and family but there are those that have influenced my poetry and so this is the space for those people, though the amount of people who've kept me alive and inspired is limitless.

Walter- Who inspired many of these poems and who taught me what it meant to love in poetry. I don't think I would've become a love poet if I hadn't met you. Thank you for leaving me with that gift.

Rich- An amazing father, friend, and artist. Thank you for all of the artwork you created for this book and for all my creative projects. Thank you for being the ear that always listens to my dreams and believes in them just as much as I do. I'm lucky to build with you in all the ways that we do.

Ray, Pedro, and Hector- Thank you for bringing your love for Anarchism into my life and practice. The conversations and experiences I've shared with you all ended up influencing this book in very big ways. This book is my way of planting a black flag on the moon.

Sandra Cisneros- I read your book Caramelo and it was there where I read the word Chicano for the first time. My mind exploded on that one summer bus ride coming from the library and I've followed the lifestyle that comes with that word ever since. Thank you for being a forever influence and Chicana icon. Thank you for being an early example of the life that could one day be possible for me.

Brenda Vaca- Miss publisher lady. Thank you for believing in my potential and for giving Mariaposa a home with Riot of Roses. I don't plan on letting you down.

Thank you to Anastasia Helena Fenald and Annalicia Aguilar for editing my work. This is their first book with editing credits and I hope you girls have many more. Good luck on your journey!

A Chicano handshake for Jose Olivarez- Thank you for writing a blurb for this book and for being one of my biggest inspirations as a Chicano poet. When I see your success it makes me so happy- one of US made it! Thank you for coming back for me and helping me in a very real way.

Meliza Banales (Missy Fuego)- Thank you for being my first poet elder/ mentor/ guide. Thank you for taking a bunch of baby Chicana feminist under your wing to make sure we continued on our road of rage and liberation. I will always consider you a big influence for me as a poet and organizer.

Thank you to Yesika Salgado for always gifting me with free seats to your workshops and for all your influence as the bad ass brown poet that you are.

Special shout out to Agua of Milpa-

The whole band is an influence of mine but I will say that I love and respect you as an OG organizer and artist. I won't forget how I went to your solo show and it brought me back to myself. It reminded me that I wanted to live my whole life the way you do- a life where art grows through every crack of concrete.

Thank you to Xela with an X: Without you there wouldn't have been La Concha and La Concha in Boyle Heights is where I read my first poems. Let that be remembered. Thank you for your sacrifice.I appreciate and respect you.

Shout out to the brother Ceasar K Avelar over at Cafe con Libros-Thank you for holding it down with Obsidian Tongues open mic all these many years and for loving on the poetry community with your heart of gold. When I think of poets I admire, you are one of them.

Brenna - Thank you for being my therapist at one of the darkest times of my life. I'm not the girl who is afraid of my own mind anymore- these poems are examples of the playground my thoughts live in now. Thank you for helping me stay alive long enough to find my way back there.

Special shout out to my sisters, my parents, to Erick and lil Gaby. Special shout out to Yasmin and her family and to my family and to all my friends that feel like blood. Shout out to my amiga Alex Beehive and her family. Shout out to my old crew over at Con Fuerza Collective.

Shout out to Tio's Tacos - which in my opinion is the most beautiful place in the I.E The whole segment Maria y el Mar was inspired by a break up and the beautiful art of Martin Sanchez . I love you Tio's Tacos.

Thank you to all my poetic influences and to all my poetic friends. There are too many for me to write here but they know who they are.

Thank you to my brother Evaristo, who is also a poet and who helped edit some of my work in the early stages. I'm grateful to be related to you in blood and poetry.

Thank you to some special spaces where I've read some poems: Espacio 1839 , La Concha, Creative Grounds, Garcia Center for the Arts, Barrio Fuerza, and Cafe con Libros have all been favorite spots of mine.

Thank you to Michael Beserra from Multimedia Militia/ SOUNDWORKS - the only non- poet I know who loves on poetry the way the poets do. He's recording all of the Chicano/ brown/ L.A Poets and keeping us alive. Keep track of this man. He's preserving Spoken word in such an important way. Thank you Michael for recording me!

I love all the artists and weirdos. The poets, the anarchists, the indigi- revolutionaries, the herbalists, the musicians, the doulas, the organizers. When the pandemic hit we all learned that a life without the art's could be possible but would surely be unbearable.

Thank you to everyone who supports me and my poetry. May we stay enraged because this is our flame. May we continue believing that a different world is possible! Let us stay ignited.The work never ends!

ABOUT THE AUTHOR

Alma Rosa Azul is a Mexican Militant who uses her pen as her rifle. Her influences range from the sweet soul lyrics of artists like Smokey Robinson to the political verses of Rage against the Machine and Bambu DePistola. She considers herself a Chicana Cubist Poet partially because her poems are constructed in a quilt-like fashion with a variety of images and influences from different places. She loves all things classic- including vintage clothing and classic Chicana literature like *The House on Mango Street* and *Chicana Falsa*. She is a bus stopper, a thrift shopper, a strong brown woman, a community organizer and a jokester in her everyday life. She is Alma Rosa Azul, a name in three parts to braid and then tie at the end with a poem.

ABOUT THE PUBLISHER

Riot of Roses Publishing House was founded in 2021 specifically to amplify the stories of historically silenced voices and narratives.

Xicana owned. Mujerista focused. For the people.

We publish books that heal and liberate.

Read our rebellion.

Find & follow us @riotofrosespublishing

Visit us at www.riotofrosespublishinghouse.com

RIOT OF ROSES
PUBLISHING HOUSE
SEJATNGA
UNCEDED TONGVA TERRITORY
SOUTH WHITTIER, CALIFORNIA